LOVE
in
ACTION

Michael C. Armour

**COLLEGE PRESS
PUBLISHING COMPANY**
Joplin, Missouri

All Scripture quotations, unless otherwise noted, are from the
New American Standard Bible, © 1960, 1962, 1963, 1968, 1971,
1972, 1973, 1975, and 1977 by The Lockman Foundation,
and are used by permission

Cover design by James D. Suiter

International Standard Book Number 0-89900-720-1

CONTENTS

STUDIES FOR SMALL GROUPS

Welcome to the *Studies for Small Groups* series from College Press. This series is designed for simplicity of use while giving insight into important issues of the Christian life. Some, like the present volume, are topical studies. Others examine a passage of Scripture for the day-to-day lessons we can learn from it.

A number of possible uses could be made of this study. Because there are a limited number of lessons, the format is ideal for new or potential Christians who can begin the study without feeling that they are tied into an overly long commitment. It could also be used for one or two months of weekly studies by a home Bible study group. The series is suitable for individual as well as group study.

Of course, any study is only as good as the effort you put into it. The group leader should study each lesson carefully before the group study session, and if possible, come up with additional Scriptures and other supporting material. Although study questions are provided for each lesson, it would also be helpful if the leader can add his or her own questions.

Neither is it necessary to complete a full lesson in one class period. If the discussion is going well, don't feel that you have to cut it off to fit time constraints, as long as the discussion is related to the topic and not off on side issues.

Because ethics is such a vital, yet controversial subject, College Press is happy to present this new 13-lesson study in the *Studies for Small Groups* series, *Love in Action*.

LOVE IN ACTION

Imitations of love come in a thousand flavors — shallow misrepresentations, even perverse ones, all passing themselves off as the real thing. As Christians, unfortunately, we sometimes settle for the counterfeits ourselves.

In fact, this study grew out of counseling experiences with lifelong members of the church who thought they were practicing love, when in fact they had given themselves to a counterfeit. These were people who had heard countless sermons and exhortations about love. But they understood it only at a doctrinal or conceptual level. They had failed (or never learned how) to translate the ideals of love into practical, "rubber-meets-the-road" habits of the heart. No one had ever helped them understand love in the context of demanding, everyday realities.

That's why I wrote *Love In Action* some 25 years ago. It was originally intended for an adult Bible school program in my congregation. I've since taught it in a half-dozen churches. In each of those instances, Christians have been excited about the insights they gained from it. They tell me that *Love In Action* has been life-changing, in the fullest sense of the word. I've even had people say that, ten years after going through *Love In Action*, they regularly reread it to stay focused on what love really means.

Now, through the kind assistance of College Press, *Love In Action* is being given an opportunity to have a broader audience. In the sections ahead we will look at love in simple language, as appropriate for the newcomer to faith as for the one who has served the Lord for years. Every chapter takes you behind the language of love to the psychological and spiritual structures that must be respected if love is to attain full maturity.

For example, how do faith, hope, and love interrelate to one another? Or again, how do faith and love provide the vehicle for conquering fear? Or how does love guide our decision when we must make a choice in which our options seem to violate some aspect of God's law? These are the kinds of issues that *Love In Action* will guide you through. The discussion questions at the end of each chapter require further, challenging reflection on the principles just reviewed. I pray that *Love In Action* will be as meaningful for your life as it has been for others over many years.

O N E

THOU *SHALT* LOVE

When it comes to moral issues, the Lord never resorts to ornate or complicated phrases. Instead, He gets right to the point. Take the way He talks about love, for instance. His language is insistent and uncompromising: "Thou SHALT love!" At our boldest we might say that we *should* love. Or that we *ought* to love. But when God obligates us to love, He dismisses polite exhortations. Instead, He makes a straightforward, no-nonsense demand: Thou SHALT love!

Some would argue that God has required the impossible. How can He *command* us to love? For that matter, how can *any* emotion be commanded? Emotions have a mind of their own. And no matter how often I might be ordered to do so, I could never feel for my neighbor — and especially my enemy — what I feel for my family and for myself!

THE AFFECTIONS OF JESUS

We must recognize, therefore, that God has never required us to have the same *feeling* toward all men. Even Jesus Himself, the One who loved perfectly, had stronger *feelings* for some men than for others. That is why we know John as "the disciple whom the Lord loved" (John 20:2). A bond existed between these two that Jesus did not share with other followers.

Does this mean that Jesus was a respecter of persons? Not at all. *He loved all men as Himself. But as a human being, He could not escape strong emotional attachments to certain people.* English translators, unfortunately, seldom distinguish between the unique love that Jesus had for John and the love that He had (and commands us to have) for all men. First-century readers could make those distinctions because the Greek language had a variety of words for love, each connoting a particular aspect of love.

VARIETIES OF LOVE

They used *eros*, for example, to refer to the physiological and passionate side of love, or what we might call sexual love. *Eros* could describe either heterosexual or homosexual relationships and was a common term in the fertility cults of Roman society. Within those cults Eros, venerated under a number of names, was worshipped with prostitution, fornication, and sodomy. This religious perversion of man's natural erotic instinct was perhaps the reason the New Testament, while teaching plainly about sexuality, never uses the word *eros*.

The Greeks had another word, *storge* (pronounced "store-gay"), for the love that ties families together. *Storge* is the love a parent has for a child, as well as the reciprocal love of children for their parents. Perhaps we could best describe *storge* as instinctual love. Arising from the very nature of family life, *storge* connoted deep affection.

> Jesus loved all men as Himself. But as a human being, He could not escape strong emotional attachments to certain people.

Intensive feelings were also associated with *philia* (pronounced "feel-eya"), the kind of love that develops between close friends. Our word "cherish" closely approximates what the Greeks meant by *philia*. Whereas *eros* was sexual love and *storge* was instinctual love, *philia* brought to mind the emotional

10

aspects of love. This was the type of love which Jesus had for Lazarus and for John (John 11:3, 36; 20:2). Jesus Himself used the term *philia* when He spoke of those who loved the praises of men (Matthew 6:5; Luke 20:46) and those who love this life (John 12:25).

Yet, of all the occurrences of love in the New Testament, *philia* appears less than two dozen times, and *storge* (always in compound with another term) is quite rare. In all other instances the word for love is *agape* (pronounced "ah-gah-pay"). And it is also *agape* that Paul describes in the immortal language of 1 Corinthians 13.

MY NEIGHBOR'S PERSPECTIVE

Notice, however, that 1 Corinthians 13 speaks neither of the passion of *eros*, the instincts of *storge*, nor the emotion of *philia*. Instead, it discusses love in terms of patience, endurance, kindness, graciousness, hope, and belief. *The virtues associated with* agape *thus flow from the mind, from the will, not the emotions.*

We might describe *agape* as an active and genuine *concern* for the well-being of the one loved. "Concern" originally meant "seeing with" (from the Latin verb *cernere*, to see). We are concerned for someone when we "see things with him." And that is what *agape* is all about: seeing things as my neighbor sees them. When I have genuinely "put myself in his shoes," when I have come to understand his perspective and sensitivities, then and only then am I ready to ask love's fundamental question: how would I want to be treated in such a situation?

AGAPE IN ACTION

What God commanded, then, is not how I should *feel* toward my enemy, but how I should *act* toward him. On occasion *agape* demands that I harness my natural feelings and go against my emotions. For that reason we consider *agape* the

11

most noble form of love. Unlike *eros, storge,* or *philia,* which are spurred by impulse, *agape* overrides impulse and inclination to do what duty, not emotion demands.

To see this distinction, imagine a house afire and two men standing outside. One is the owner of the home, the other a passer-by. Suddenly the homeowner's child dashes back inside the house to save a pet. Without hesitation both the father and the passer-by rush into the flames, searching frantically for the youngster.

Both of these men are obviously doing the "loving thing," but they are acting from different kinds of love. A normal instinctual response underlies the father's efforts. Because his offspring is endangered, he is pushed into action. But the stranger's instincts and emotions tell him to stay away from the fire, that he has nothing to gain and everything to lose in the flames. Yet *agape,* his duty as a neighbor, quenches the impulse of his emotions and prompts him to join the rescue.

This is why *agape* is love of the highest order. Only *agape* violates the dictates of instinct and moves us to act out of regard for our neighbor. And this is the noble perspective for which the Lord was calling when he said, "Thou *shalt* love."

REFLECTING ON LESSON ONE

1. Is it possible to have both *agape* love and *philia* love toward the same individual? If so, do these two kinds of love ever come in conflict with one another?

2. One of the few appearances of *storge* in the New Testament is found in Romans 12:10; "Be devoted (*philostorgoi*) to one another in brotherly love (*philadelphia*)." Note how Paul brings together both the concept of *storge* love and *philia* love in this same passage. How does one go about developing these types of affection for other members of the church?

3. When Paul said, "Love never fails" (1 Corinthians 13:8), he used *agape*. Could he have used *eros, storge,* or *philia* just as well?

4. Since the Bible avoids the word *eros*, are we to conclude that Scripture frowns on erotic love? What are some ways in which *agape* may place restraints on eroticism?

5. Read Ephesians 5:22-23. There Paul describes the love that should govern Christian marriage, and he uses the word *agape*. What implication does that have for the couple that says, "We are getting a divorce because we don't love each other any more"?

6. Since "sympathy" means "suffering with," is it possible truly to sympathize with someone for whom I have no emotional (*philia*) love?

7. Read John 21:15-17. In that passage Jesus asks Peter three times, "Do you love me?" The first two times Jesus asks if Peter has *agape* love for Him. In both instances Peter answers that he has *philia* love for Jesus. Finally Jesus asks if Peter has *philia* love, with Peter answering that he does. In your opinion, what is the significance of that interchange?

2
T W O

THE OBLIGATION TO LOVE

While other religions praise love as a virtue, Christianity *demands* it as an obligation. As we noted in the opening chapter, this demand governs not so much how I *feel* toward my neighbor, but how I *act* toward him. Do I offer wealthy men prominent seats, but make a footstool of the poor? Do I give lip service to feeding the hungry, but rarely hand them even a morsel? Do I call for clothing the naked, but refuse to part with coat and shirt? Am I content to pass blissfully along the road, leaving wounded and bleeding men to their fate? These are the questions that test love's presence. And they are all questions centered in action.

THE GREATEST LOVE

Thus, when Jesus singled out the highest expression of love, it was love in action He described. "Greater love has no one than this, that one lay down his life for his friends" (John 15:13). John later pointed to the same principle, saying that the self-sacrificing demonstration of Christ's love obligates us to love our fellow man. "We know love by this," John wrote, "that He laid down His life for us; and we ought to lay down our lives for the brethren" (1 John 3:16). The striking thing about Jesus' love is that He manifested it toward us

14

when we were so unlovely. "One will hardly die for a *righteous* man," Paul told the Romans, "though perhaps for a good man *someone* would even dare to die. But God demonstrates His love for us in that while we were yet *sinners*, Christ died for us" (Romans 5:7-8).

LOVING THE UNLOVELY

If Christ, then, died for me when I was so unlovely, what duty do I have toward my neighbor, especially toward my "unlovely" neighbor? Can I use his unattractiveness as an excuse to ignore his needs? Am I justified in "writing him off" because of his spiritual and social ugliness? Obviously not. One of the worst tyrants in all of Christ's parables was the unforgiving servant (Matthew 18:23-34). He, like us, was a great debtor before his lord. Again like us, he received his lord's grace. His debt (worth about $10,000,000) was canceled. How unthinkable that this same man, having been relieved from such indebtedness, would then be unwilling to forgive a man who owed him less than twenty dollars!!

We feel no inclination to defend the unforgiving servant. Rational minds have nothing to offer in his defense. Every law of decency calls for those who receive mercy to show mercy themselves. Nor may we discriminate, saying, "I will show mercy to this person, but not to that one." God's universal love obligates us to love universally ourselves. Indeed, if I love selectively, I am essentially "authorizing" God to be selective in His forgiveness of me; for Jesus taught His disciples to pray, "Father, forgive us our trespasses *as we forgive those who trespass against us*" (Matthew 6:12).

My ability to forgive is a good barometer of my love. Forgiveness means giving up a claim for requital. Forgiveness is another instance in which love governs not so much the way I *feel* toward a person, but how I *act* toward that person.

Some have said that to forgive we must also forget. The only problem is, "forgive and forget" just doesn't work.

15

Experience indicates that the harder I try to forget something, the more tenaciously it embeds itself in memory. Thus, I may find it impossible to *forget* what someone has done. But I am still obligated to *forgive*.

COVERING A MULTITUDE OF SINS

Forgiveness means treating someone as though proper repayment has been made. When a loan is forgiven, the lender acts as though repayment has been made in full, even though the borrower failed in his responsibilities. Under ancient law anyone committing a crime was presumed to incur a debt to his or her victim. That victim was to receive restitution for the wrong done.

In the same way, people who sin against me today become, in a sense, indebted to me. When I forgive them, I act as though repayment has been made, as though the required restitution has been "given for" the wrong. I may not be able to forget what they did, but I can *treat* them as though all accounts have been settled. The greater the forgiveness, the greater the love. And when love is full grown, it "covers a multitude of sins" (1 Peter 4:8). *That is, it continues to forgive, even when sinned against repeatedly.*

Interestingly, the less I love someone *emotionally* the more *agape* I may need in order to forgive. It is somewhat natural to forgive close friends and family, those we call our "loved ones." It is far less natural to forgive people with whom we have no emotional attachment. As a rule our ability to forgive (and thus the magnitude of our *agape*) comes when we can forgive even the most unlovely stranger who has done us an injustice.

THE UNIQUENESS OF CHRISTIAN LOVE

Full-grown love continues to forgive, even when sinned against repeatedly.

Forgiveness is but one of many ways in which we are "obligated" to love. As we have already seen, we also have an obligation to minister to needs, even to

16

lay down life itself, should the need arise. *But one of the most frequent tests of love is the recurring opportunity to forgive.* In this, as in all other activities of love, Jesus is our example. While we were yet sinners, while we were yet His enemy, Christ died to forgive us. It is that pattern of Jesus' love that makes Christianity unique. Christianity was not the first religion to single out love as praiseworthy. Hymns to the beauty of love adorn virtually every advanced religion. How, then, can Christianity claim to be the religion of love? It does so because it embraces what no other religion can offer: Jesus Christ Himself as the example of love.

NOT OBLIGATION, BUT OPPORTUNITY

The deeper our comprehension of His love, the greater our appreciation for it. With that appreciation comes an enlarged sense of our own obligation to love. In expecting us to love, God has required nothing of us that He has not already done Himself. We are to forgive seventy times seven because God has forgiven us far more than that. We are to lay down our lives for others because Jesus has laid down His life for us. We are to love the unlovely and undesirable because God showed His greatest love for us even while we were immersed in the ugliness of sin.

Once we recognize how greatly God has loved us, once we see his eagerness to forgive, we no longer resent God's having obligated us to love. We are instead infused with such happiness and unspeakable joy that love and forgiveness become our second nature. No longer do we think of the "obligation" to love. Instead, we rejoice in the *opportunity* to show our gratitude for what God has done.

REFLECTING ON LESSON TWO

1. Suggest some ways in which my ability to forgive serves as a barometer of my love.

2. Is it always easier to forgive friends and family members than to forgive strangers and casual acquaintances? Why or why not?

3. What are the traits in people that make it most difficult to love them? To forgive them?

4. Someone has said, "Only in the love of those who do not serve a purpose, love begins to unfold." What does that statement mean? Do you agree?

5. Read Luke 12:48. How does the principle laid down in the last half of this verse relate to our obligation to love?

6. What counsel would you give someone who wants to forgive another, but finds it impossible to overcome the deep hurt that resulted from the other person's actions?

7. Read the following verses from 1 John. These all deal with our obligation to love. Indicate beside each of the following passages the reason it gives for our having a responsibility to love.
   a. 1 John 3:10-12
   b. 1 John 3:16
   c. 1 John 3:23
   d. 1 John 4:7
   e. 1 John 4:10-11
   f. 1 John 4:19
   g. 1 John 4:20-21
   h. 1 John 5:1-3

3

NOW ABIDETH THESE THREE

In Christianity love is the queen of the virtues. But standing alongside her are two constant attendants, faith and hope. These three — faith, hope, and love — are so interdependent that in this world love cannot exist apart from the other two.

Paul makes this strikingly clear when we analyze love in action in 1 Corinthians 13. There he describes love in terms of kindness, graciousness, patience, and endurance, each of them a kinsman of hope. Or to put it another way, hopeless people have little to do with kindness, graciousness, or patience. Hopeless people are so preoccupied with themselves and their personal misfortune that they have no time to recognize the needs of others, to hold out a helping hand. In short, they have no time for love.

The very word "hopeless," in fact, suggests resignation, withdrawal, and retreat from courageous action. But why does bravery disappear when hope vanishes? Why is boldness so rare among hopeless people? The answer is found in the fact that hopeless people have lost faith — faith either in themselves, in their cause, or in their compatriots. Thus, where there is no faith, there is no hope. And where there is no hope, people are unlikely to manifest the attributes of love.

THE SUBSTANCE OF HOPE

Hebrews 11:1 shows us why faith and hope are inseparable. Do you recall the familiar reading of this verse in the King James Version? Faith, it says, is the substance of things hoped for, the evidence of things not seen. "Substance" means "that which stands under." (The Greek term *hypostasis* used in this verse has exactly the same literal meaning.) *Faith, then, is what "stands under" our hope. Or to put it another way, faith undergirds hope.*

But what "stands under" our faith? Is it nothing more than wishful thinking, as some have supposed? Or does it have a foundation? The biblical answer is plain. Faith rests on evidence, evidence of an "unseen world." As we shall see in chapter four, Christianity is a "reason-able" religion. That is, its basic tenets can be supported by rational arguments (1 Peter 3:15). So Hebrews 11:1 might be summarized as saying that our hope stands on faith that itself rests on a foundation of underlying evidence.

In day-to-day conversation we sometimes touch on this faith-hope relationship in a telling way. Consider, for example, two men sitting at a country club, waiting for a third man. The three were to meet at 9 a.m. for a round of golf. It is now 9:15.

"Shall we just give up and start without him?" one man asks. "No," the other replies. "He assured me he would be here, and I am confident he will show up."

"Is he generally a man of his word?"

"Oh, absolutely. He has never failed to keep a promise to me. And all our mutual friends insist that his integrity is above question. I have complete faith in him."

> Faith is what "stands under" our hope. Or to put it another way, faith undergirds hope.

Notice what their dialogue reveals. They have every *hope* of playing golf with him today. Why? Because of their *faith* in his word. And what is the basis of that faith? The fact — or evidence — that he is a man who keeps his promise.

WAITING PATIENTLY

It is a sure sign that we have given up hope when we begin to say, "I can't wait any more."

So the golfers wait, confident that their partner will arrive soon. Another 15 minutes go by. Then 30 minutes. Finally the clock reaches 10 a.m. Will they continue to wait? Perhaps. But eventually they will lose faith in their friend's promise. When that faith erodes, they will say, "We had hoped to play golf with him, but we cannot wait any longer."

This leads to a further observation. *It is a sure sign that we have given up hope when we begin to say, "I can't wait any more."* Impatience is a hallmark of hopelessness. (Note Paul's reference to this principle in Romans 8:25.) Hopeless men simply cannot wait. They must live for the here-and-now. They have no confidence in the future. They have lost faith that promises will be kept. They must pursue the "right now" and pursue it so uncompromisingly that they become selfish, pushy, and indulgent. Their actions become the works of the flesh, not the fruit of the Spirit (Galatians 5:19-23). And before long, utter chaos ensues. Hopeless, impatient people find it impossible to act lovingly.

A HOPELESS WORLD

One could argue, indeed, that the current moral turmoil in Western society is due to an absence of faith. Not only has faith in God declined, the world has also generally lost faith in government, in education, in big business, in big labor, in everything. When people no longer feel they have anything to believe in, they lose hope and resort to violence and destruction. Their language becomes vulgar and blasphemous, their literature obscene and pornographic. Why? Because they are venting the frustration brought on by a hopeless situation.

Private conversation again illustrates this principle. So long as we hope to get our point across, we speak patiently and in calm tones. But when it appears that we are being ignored, our tone changes. Our voice rises in pitch and becomes more insistent. When we give up hope that we will get an honest hearing from the other party, we resort to shouting and throwing things. We yell, "LISTEN TO ME!!" We may even adorn our "listen to me" with profanity, if not outright obscenity. On a much larger scale, society today is doing the same sort of thing, venting its hopelessness and spewing out vulgarity on every side.

What man needs, therefore, is something to believe in. Collectively and individually we need a foundation of faith. Only when that foundation has been laid do our lives have meaning, a meaning that gives substance to our hope. Then, and only then, are the fruits of love possible. A popular song in the '70s said, "What the world needs now is love." But before love is possible, the world needs something — or Someone — to believe in.

REFLECTING ON LESSON THREE

1. We tend to use "hope" and "wishful thinking" inter-changeably, as when we say, "I know we don't have much of a chance, but I sure hope our team wins the championship this year." Are hope and wishful thinking one and the same? If not, how do they differ?

2. In 1 Corinthians 13, where Paul discusses faith, hope, and love, he says, "Love is eternal." Are faith and hope also eternal?

3. Explain what Paul means in Romans 8:24-25 when he writes, "Hope that is seen is not hope." And what does he mean when he says, "We are saved in hope"?

4. Read Hebrews 11:17-19. Describe how faith and hope were intermixed in this incident from Abraham's life.

5. Read Romans 4:17-22. What does Paul mean when he says that "Abraham hoped against hope"?

6. After studying Romans 5:1-5, explain how patience working through experience produces hope. What does Paul mean by the statement, "Hope maketh not ashamed"? (This is the rendering of the King James Version.)

7. Look at Romans 15:4 and explain how our understanding of the Old Testament produces hope. Is the study of the Old Testament really that important for Christians?

8. List some events in contemporary society that suggest man's hopelessness.

4

THE FIRST AND GREAT COMMAND

When it comes to loving God, we must not go halfway. Loving Him is to consume every breath and every moment of life. "You shall love the Lord your God with all your heart, and with all your soul, and with all your mind, and with all your strength." That, Jesus said, is the first and great command (Mark 12:28-31). From this one principle all other principles of spiritual living flow. Our love for God is the rationale on which we base not only our moral behavior, but our Christian worship and service, as well. Thus, when love for God is imperfect, spirituality is imperfect.

ALL YOUR HEART

That is why the first requirement for loving God is to love Him with all my HEART. In a word, I am to love Him *wholeheartedly*. There must be no hypocrisy or divided loyalty in my love. Such halfheartedness spells disappointment, if not disaster. When I love God only halfheartedly, my spiritual life stumbles along. Half-committed to the world and only partially committed to God, I suffer from spiritual schizophrenia. The New Testament, in fact, warns about such double-mindedness. A double-minded man is unstable in all his ways, James wrote. Then he added, "Don't let that man expect to

24

receive anything from the Lord" (James 1:7-8, author's paraphrase).

Our singularity of heart is made necessary by the oneness of God. The "first and great command" was prefaced by these words: "Hear, O Israel, the LORD is our God, the LORD is one!" (Deuteronomy 6:4-5; Mark 12:29-30). The implication is that *since God is constant and unchanging, those who walk with Him must also be constant and unchanging.* Their lives must manifest singleness of love and character. Since there is no darkness in God (1 John 1:5), those who walk with Him must be "delivered from the domain of darkness" (Colossians 1:13). It is the "love of darkness" that prevents people from accepting Christ (John 1:19); and so long as any love for darkness remains within us, we are not loving God wholeheartedly.

> Since God is constant and unchanging, those who walk with Him must also be constant and unchanging.

ALL YOUR SOUL

On the other hand, once we come to love God wholeheartedly, we are ready to sacrifice everything for Him. That includes our very lives. Such is the meaning of loving God with all your *soul*. As used here, "soul" means the "life principle" in man. We must love God more than life itself. Some men will be so eager to save their lives that they will lose true life, Jesus warned. But others, because they are willing to lay down their lives for God, will find an even richer life in Him (John 12:25). On another occasion the Lord put it this way: "Be faithful unto death [i.e., even when threatened with death itself] and I will give you the crown of life" (Revelation 2:10).

ALL YOUR MIND

The possibility of martyrdom, of course, is the ultimate test of whether we are willing to live completely under the lordship of Christ. But before we can weather that test, we must resolve in our own minds any doubt about our destiny and the hereafter. We must have followed Peter's advice and prepared ourselves with a reason for the hope that is within us (1 Peter 3:15). Hopeless people cannot face the thought of martyrdom. They will compromise before they accept a hopeless death. And so it is that we must work out our convictions carefully, supporting our confidence in Christianity by searching for substantiating evidence. In short, we must love the Lord with all our *mind*.

INTELLECTUAL PRIDE

At this very point, indeed, Satan reclaims many of us. Knowing our tendency toward intellectual pride, he uses that weakness to drive wedges between us and God. *From the dawn of creation Satan has recognized that pride is potentially deadly, and that intellectual pride is perhaps the deadliest of all.* In bringing about the very first sin, Satan depicted the fruit as desirable to make one wise (Genesis 3:6). Through the desire for wisdom Satan weakened Eve's loyalty to God. And once she quit loving God wholeheartedly, sin prevailed.

This is not to suggest that Christianity is anti-intellectual. To the contrary, God calls on us to serve Him with *all* our mind. To allow Satan even a toehold in our minds is to risk opening ourselves entirely to sin. Our learning must underscore man's imperfection and his ultimate powerlessness to direct his own steps. It must yield humility rather than arrogance. It must point beyond the handiwork of men to the handiwork of heaven. It must take men and women from total dependence on themselves to total dependence on their Maker.

From the dawn of creation Satan has recognized that pride is potentially deadly, and that intellectual pride is perhaps the deadliest of all.

ALL YOUR STRENGTH

It is one thing, however, to give lip service to dependence on God, quite another to turn life over to Him completely. While we are willing to put *much* of our life under God's direction, we tend to retain a certain amount of independent control for ourselves. But we must not "compartmentalize" our lives, putting God in charge of some compartments, while keeping other rooms under our own control. God must permeate *all* our activity, must direct *all* our steps. Or to say it the way Jesus did, we must love God with all our *strength*.

There is no room in Christian speech for such statements as "business is business" or "politics is politics." Those words indicate that we have sectioned off our lives like an apartment complex. In some of those apartments godliness may hold sway. But in others any mention of Christian ethics or spiritual values would be inappropriate and irrelevant.

When that occurs, we must remember that our bodies are not an apartment complex, but a temple, a temple for God's indwelling (1 Corinthians 6:19; Ephesians 2:19-22). And God's indwelling can no more limit itself to part of our lives than His presence can limit itself to a mere corner of the universe.

REFLECTING ON LESSON FOUR

1. When Jesus said that there is a "first and great command," was He suggesting that certain commands are more important than others? Was He saying that some virtues are more important than others?

2. Why do you think loving God is the "first and great command"?

3. In Revelation 2:10 Jesus said, "Be faithful unto death . . . ." Is that the same thing as saying, "Be faithful until death . . . ."?

4. What did Jesus mean when He said, "Those who would save their life will lose it; and those who would lose their life will save it"?

5. Some people say, "I would give up *anything* for Christ." Others say, "I would give up *everything* for Christ." What is the practical difference between these two statements? If you were called on to give up everything for Christ, what would be the most difficult things for you to part with?

6. What three biblical characters do you think most perfectly kept the "first and great command"? Explain your choices.

7. Is intellectual pride the most deadly type of pride? Give some examples of how intellectual pride can separate us from God.

8. The Jews never developed a word for "secular," for they felt that a man's religion encompassed his entire life. Do you agree or disagree with that position?

9. What do you personally find to be the greatest obstacle in trying to love God with all your heart, soul, strength, and mind?

5
F I V E

HOW BIG IS THE NEIGHBORHOOD?

When Jesus talked about loving our neighbors, His hearers wanted to know, "How big is the neighborhood?" Or to put the question in their terms, "Who is my neighbor?" (Luke 10:29.) Jesus answered with the parable of the good Samaritan, concluding with the question, "Who acted neighborly in this story?" (Luke 10:30-36.) Jesus thus put the emphasis where it should be, not on who my neighbor is, but on what it means to act neighborly.

RESPONSE-ABILITY

Yet, in the process of defining neighborliness, Jesus left no doubt about the boundaries of the neighborhood. He described those boundaries in terms of response-ability, my ability to respond. My neighbor is not determined by spatial proximity, but by my capability to meet needs. Whenever people have needs to which I can minister, they become people to whom I have a response-ability. The degree to which I carry out that response-ability determines the quality of my neighborliness.

Once I view neighborliness in this way, all geographic, national, and racial boundaries become transparent. It now becomes possible to act neighborly toward strangers, foreigners, even enemies. This enlarged sense of neighborhood also forces my neighborliness to shed its temporal boundaries. I suddenly realize that I have neighborly responsibilities to generations yet unborn. The way I conduct my affairs today, the way in which I use or abuse God's creation, will directly affect the quality of life for future generations. Thus, *people who will not even exist during my own lifetime are potentially my neighbors.*

THE NEAR-DWELLERS

Originally the word "neighbor" meant "the one who lives nearby." (It comes from an Anglo-Saxon term meaning "the near-dweller.") Neighborliness should be studied first, therefore, in terms of my response-ability toward those who are near at hand. Since those are the people with whom I have the most frequent contact, it is among them that I most often find needs to which I could minister. But the "near-dwellers" are sometimes the hardest people to act "neighborly" toward. Their proximity puts continual demands on my time, my energy, my patience. Eventually my own selfish nature comes to resent their demands. At that point I begin looking for justifiable ways to avoid my responsibility toward them.

Commonly I evade this responsibility by refusing to focus on their needs. I would rather talk of starving people in India or Africa than of hungry people in my own city. I would rather talk about racial problems in South Africa or in some distant ghetto than about my duty to the minority family down the block. In short, I prefer to talk about needs that are far-removed from my front door. By focusing on distant needs, I can excuse myself for being inactive in the battle against want and suffering. I can tell myself, "I am really concerned, but there is just nothing I can do about such great problems when they are so far away."

But am I genuinely concerned? Isn't this just a game I play with myself?

> People who will not even exist during my own lifetime are potentially my neighbors.

30

Isn't my refusal to see the needs of people nearby demonstration enough that I am basically unconcerned and unneighborly?

ACTING NEIGHBORLY

The acid test of neighborliness, then, is not my kind words, but my caring involvement. To make a paraphrase of James' language, we can say, "Show me your neighborliness without works, and I by my work will show you my neighborliness." James himself noted that neighborliness is either active or it is meaningless. "If a brother or sister is without clothing and in need of daily food, and one of you says to them, 'Go in peace, be warmed and filled'; and yet you do not give them what is necessary for their body; what use is that?" (James 2:15-16.)

Jesus, too, warned in His parables that a pivotal issue at the Judgment will be whether one's sense of neighborliness produced appropriate fruit. Some will hear Him say, "Depart from me, accursed ones . . . for I was hungry and you gave Me nothing to eat; I was thirsty and you gave Me nothing to drink; I was a stranger and you did not invite Me in; naked and you did not clothe Me; sick, and in prison, and you did not visit Me" (Matthew 25:41-43). Nor did He accept the excuse, "We did not see the need." Instead He insisted that failure to see and meet the needs of people the world dismisses as insignificant is the same as refusing to minister to Christ Himself.

SPECIAL NEIGHBORS

Another way we sometimes evade our neighborly responsibility is by refusing to recognize certain people as neighbors. This is particularly true when it comes to our families. We tend to think of the neighborhood as "out there," starting at a point beyond my front yard. But in the Christian sense of the term, we have a neighborly relationship with our husbands, our wives, our children, our parents, our brothers, our sis-

31

ters. As someone has suggested, *my wife is first my neighbor and only secondly my wife.*

Our failure to recognize the "neighborliness" which attends family life has led to a needless unhappiness in our homes. We will say things and do things to our family that we would never say or do to a "neighbor." We prove by our action that we have excluded our family from our sense of neighborhood. But the accident of kinship in no way diminishes my duty to see my family first as neighbors and only secondly as family. My love for them must first be governed by *agape*, only secondarily by *storge* or *philia*. Unless I see my family as part of the neighborhood that I am to "love as myself," I may treat them shamefully, saying all along, "I love you."

DIMENSIONS OF THE NEIGHBORHOOD

The neighborhood, then, is expansive indeed. It begins not at my curb or at my front door, but at my fireside. It encompasses every member of my family, includes every person who dwells nearby, and finally encircles everyone with needs to which I have the ability to respond. I must always be aware of both the inner and outer dimension of my neighborhood. I must be forever enhancing my skill at seeing the neighborhood's needs, forever improving my response and my ministry to the needs that I see. This is, after all, what the second great command is all about.

My wife is first
my neighbor and
only secondly
my wife.

REFLECTING ON LESSON FIVE

1. Other than for the story of the Good Samaritan, what do you consider the two greatest examples of neighborliness in the Bible?

2. Can you cite biblical examples of men who failed to treat their family "neighborly"?

3. Are there any basic differences between our love for God and our love for our neighbor? If so, name some of those differences.

4. John says we cannot love God, whom we have not seen, if we cannot love our brother whom we *have* seen (1 John 4:20). Why is that the case?

5. Explain the significance of the word "response-ability" as used in this lesson. What is the relationship between "response-ability" and my sense of neighborliness?

6. In light of the fact that the Bible teaches that this world is but temporary and is destined for destruction, why should Christians involve themselves in environmental or ecological issues? If the world is passing away anyway, is it appropriate for Christians to spend their time on efforts to protect the ecology?

7. Can group loyalties, such as nationalism, ever work against a Christian's duty as a neighbor? If so, in what way?

8. Are Christian fellowship and Christian neighborliness one and the same thing, or are there basic differences

between them? What are their similarities? Their differences, if any?

9. Explain the meaning of the following statement: selfishness loves things and uses people; neighborliness loves people and uses things.

6

S I X

AS YOU LOVE YOURSELF

In the minds of many Christians, loving oneself is a terrible vice. To the extent that I love myself, they believe, I am unable to love others. How strange, then, that Jesus commanded us to love our neighbors *as ourselves*. He seemed to say that there is no contradiction between loving oneself and loving others. In fact, His language is such that He makes self-love a prerequisite for all other forms of love. I am not prepared to love my neighbor until I first love myself.

CHRISTIAN SELF-LOVE

Are we to assume, therefore, that Christian morality is based on selfishness? Not at all. It is based on self-love, which is quite different from selfishness. To understand that difference, however, we must first grasp the meaning of self-love.

Earlier we defined *agape* as an active and genuine concern for the well-being of the one loved. It would follow, therefore, that self-love is an active and genuine concern for our own well-being. So what did Jesus mean when He said, "Love your neighbor as yourself"? He was saying that to work for the well-being of others I need a genuine concern for myself. For one thing, I understand others primarily by referring to

35

my own experiences. I can identify with a mother and her children who are hungry, because I have felt hunger pangs myself. I can comprehend how frustration demoralizes my neighbor, because I have been demoralized by frustration, too.

Understanding myself, in other words, becomes the baseline from which I learn to understand others. That's why *self-love becomes the baseline from which I learn* to love others. I can be genuinely concerned for their well-being because I know firsthand what it means to be concerned for my personal well-being. Thus we see that self-love, far from being *opposed* to brotherly love, is in fact the *basis* of brotherly love.

IS SELF-LOVE A VIRTUE?

Or to put it another way, when I pursue my neighbor's well-being, I do so by promoting that person's happiness, health, and security. Seeing me promote that well-being, onlookers will properly conclude that I am acting in a loving way. They would properly judge my actions as moral and upright.

Why should I be considered immoral, then, when I seek happiness, health, and security for myself? If it is wrong to seek my own well-being, I have but two other alternatives. I will either have to desire unhappiness, or I will have to profess no preference whatsoever between happiness and unhappiness. But who would consider me in my right mind if I did not care whether I was happy or not?

And what of my health? If it is wrong to desire good health, then I will either have to desire ill health, or I must become someone to whom health makes no difference at all. But if a man does not care whether he is sick or well, we immediately question his mental acumen. Moreover, if he actually *desires* unhappiness, poor health, and insecurity, we hurriedly recommend a good psychiatrist! Our conclusion must therefore be that it is only sensible and moral for us to seek our own happiness, security, and health — that is, to love ourselves.

> Self-love becomes the baseline from which I learn to love others.

SELF-LOVE AND SELFISHNESS

In contrast to the selfish man, who defines himself in terms of what he *has*, the self-loving man defines himself in terms of what he *is*. He knows that happiness and mental health are possible only when such virtues as kindness, graciousness, thoughtfulness, and the ability to forgive rule his life. Yet, such virtues call for a man to focus not on himself, but on the needs of others. How can a man be gracious, thoughtful, and kind unless his attention is always attuned to the needs of those around him?

> The selfish man is not guilty of loving himself too much. Instead, he is guilty of loving himself too little.

Thus, the life of the self-loving person becomes "you-centered," whereas the life of the selfish person remains "I-centered." Paul alluded to that contrast when he wrote the Philippians, "Do nothing from selfishness or empty conceit, but with humility of mind let each of you regard one another as more important than himself; do not merely look out for your own personal interests, but also for the interests of others" (Philippians 2:3-4).

This seeking of the other person's interest has a way of safeguarding our own happiness. Someone compared happiness to a butterfly which if energetically pursued, manages to stay just out of reach. But if we go about our task, forgetting the butterfly, the creature comes suddenly to alight on our shoulder.

THE FRUITS OF SELFISHNESS

In reality, therefore, *the selfish man is not guilty of loving himself too much. Instead, he is guilty of loving himself too little.* By focusing only on himself, his own needs, and his own "things," he fills his life with unhappiness, insecurity, and the attendant evils of suspicion and jealously. If he were trying to perpetuate such unhappiness and insecurity in the life of another, bystanders would rightly conclude that he despised the other person. Doesn't it stand to reason, then,

37

that a man who perpetrates such qualities in his own life really fails to love himself? Ironically, he probably believes that he loves himself immensely.

We have all experienced the unpleasant atmosphere which surrounds selfish people. What misery and discord they spread everywhere they go! Theirs are the fruits of men and women who do not know how to love their neighbor, having never learned to love themselves. They have never discovered *true service of self, which comes from ignoring one's self and pursuing the best interest of the other person.*

The true service of self comes from ignoring one's self and pursuing the best interest of the other person.

REFLECTING ON LESSON SIX

1. Jesus said, "Love your neighbor *as yourself*." Paul, in Philippians 2:3 said, "Let each of you count the other as *more important than himself*." Was Paul contradicting Jesus? Explain why or why not.

2. Why didn't Jesus say, "Love your neighbor *more than* yourself"? Is it possible to love a neighbor *more* than yourself?

3. Explain how self-love serves as a basis for brotherly love.

4. Give a hypothetical example of how a person's selfishness might lead to a physical and/or mental breakdown.

5. Elaborate on what is meant by the statement that a selfish man does not love himself too much — he loves himself too little.

6. Jesus, the example of perfect love, has been called "the man for others" because of his "you-centered" love. Cite instances from His ministry that show Jesus as primarily interested in the well-being of others at a moment when He had reason to be preoccupied with His own immediate needs.

7. Explain how a man can have both an awareness of his sins and limitations while possessing at the same time love for himself. How can he maintain a positive self-image when he sees his shortcomings so clearly?

7
S E V E N

LOVING OR LOVABLE?

"Buy our product and everyone will love you!" How many times a day do commercials scream *that* message at us? Americans spend billions each year making themselves more attractive, more "lovable." But does all that outlay really increase their happiness? Evidently not, considering the spiraling rate of crime, divorce, and suicide. Having spent fortunes so that people will like us, why are we so miserable and unhappy?

Our misery stems from having put our emphasis in the wrong place. Happiness and meaning in life do not come from making ourselves more lovable. They come from making ourselves more *loving*. So long as my values are built around making myself lovable, I will make frequent forays into selfishness and "I-centeredness." As with other selfish people, I will define myself by what I have — good looks, smart clothes, a sharp car — and not by what I am.

MASK MAKING

But why do men and women find it necessary to focus on what they have instead of what they are? In a word, it's the problem of a poor self-image. "No one could love me for what I am," they believe. "If I am to be loved, I must make others love me for what I have."

And thus begins the pursuit of things. Unfortunately, the scheme always fails. With cosmetics, clothes, and cars I carefully construct a mask that says, "Look, world! This is what I am like." Yet I myself know differently. That's because I bump into the "real me" every morning at the bathroom mirror — before I can get my mask on!

> Without the self-confidence that a healthy self-image affords, we are unlikely to manifest true agape.

SELF-IMAGE AND AGAPE

People with poor self-images never really forget that they are wearing a mask, that they are presenting a false front to the world. Thus, even when others act lovingly toward them, the experience proves disappointing. They interpret acts of love as responses to their mask, not responses to their genuine self. "If people knew what I'm really like," they tell themselves, "they would not treat me with such regard." In effect, they feel unloved even when others treat them lovingly. The whole project to become lovable has failed.

Christians must never be indifferent to poor self-images, either in themselves or in others. *Without the self-confidence that a healthy self-image affords, we are unlikely to manifest true agape.* Our feelings of inadequacy and fears of rejection will prevent us from becoming involved meaningfully with our neighbors. Poor self-images also hamper neighborliness in another dimension, for they deter self-love, a necessary antecedent (as we saw in chapter six) to loving one's neighbor.

IMPROVING SELF-IMAGES

But how do I go about improving a weak self-image? I start by realizing the nobility of each person, including myself. God fashioned human beings initially in His own image (Genesis 1:27). Even at my worst I still bear the residual imprint of the divine image. No creature other than mankind bears that imprint. I am therefore far from insignificant. I'm one of the elites in the universe!

Secondly, I must recognize that I *can* be loved for what I am, for the Lord, who looks at my heart, not my "mask," loves me immensely (1 Samuel 16:7). *His love is never based on what I have. How could I ever amass enough "things" to impress God,* who created it all? No, God loves ME!! He loves that "real me" who stares back from the bathroom mirror each morning. God loves me for who I am *without* the mask. And what can separate me from His love? Paul posed that very question, and answered with a resounding, "Nothing!" (Romans 8:38-39.)

I AM IMPORTANT

I must also recognize how *intense* God's love is for me. While I was yet God's enemy, Christ died for ME. He died for MY reconciliation (Romans 5:6-11). God loves me so much that Christ would have died for me even if every other person in the world had been perfect. Despite my blemishes and imperfections (which God recognizes long before I do), He still thinks me IMPORTANT. I am still WANTED. I am LOVED.

This is not to suggest that Christians are egoists. They are not. The recognition of their importance is counterbalanced by another great truth, namely, that they do not deserve God's love. There is no way in which we merit the title "sons of God" (Ephesians 2:8-9). Our understanding of God's love should therefore lead to gratitude and humility, never to arrogance. Paul told Christians of his day, "Do not think of yourselves more highly than you ought" (Romans 12:3). His warning is well-taken. But we should note that he did *not* say, "Do not think of yourself highly." Paul knew that every man must recognize his own individual importance before God. Positive self-images are essential.

> God's love is never based on what I have. How could I ever amass enough "things" to impress God?

42

AWARENESS OF MY FAULTS

There is no basic incompatibility between a positive self-image and awareness of one's faults.

Nor does this recognition of my importance (and the self-esteem which comes with that recognition) cloud my vision of my own shortcomings. Paul could see his weaknesses clearly. He even referred to himself as the vilest of sinners, having persecuted the church itself (1 Corinthians 15:9; 1 Timothy 1:13; Ephesians 3:8). Nonetheless, he possessed a very positive self-image. Before King Agrippa he would say, "I wish that you and everyone in this court were just like me, except for my imprisonment" (Acts 26:29, author's paraphrase). And to his friends at Corinth he could say without hesitation, "Be imitators of me, just as I also am of Christ" (1 Corinthians 11:1).

There is no basic incompatibility, therefore, between a positive self-image and awareness of one's faults. Nor is it wrong, being aware of those faults, to work at overcoming them. Improving myself and maximizing my potential is what Christian growth is all about. But these "self-improvement projects" are not aimed at making myself more lovable. They aim at building an even stronger self-image, a self-image that encourages self-love. Only when I know how to love myself am I prepared to love my neighbor *as* myself. Christian self-improvement never centers in an effort to become more lovable. It centers instead on becoming more loving.

MADISON AVENUE AND JESUS

We can sum up the basic difference between Madison Avenue and Christ in just a few words. Madison Avenue says, "Focus on yourself." Jesus says, "Focus on others." Madison Avenue says, "Improve yourself so that others will love you." Jesus says, "Improve yourself so that as you learn to love yourself, you can love *others* more effectively." Which voice are you listening to?

REFLECTING ON LESSON SEVEN

1. In 1 Corinthians 11:1, was Paul being egotistical when he told his readers to imitate him in their spiritual lives? If he was not egotistical, how can you justify his statement?

2. What are some basic contrasts between the person who wants to become more loving and the one who seeks to be "lovable" (as that word is used in this lesson)?

3. Show how a poor self-image can lead to selfishness.

4. What biblical principles may be used to improve one's self-image?

5. Is it appropriate for people to be proud of themselves? What biblical and practical guidelines should be used to keep pride under control?

6. Many braggarts are really individuals with poor self-images. How can their bragging and boasting be caused by that self-image problem?

7. In light of what we have learned thus far, explain the following statement: "Love that calls attention to itself is not love."

8. Is it possible for any of us to live in human society without constructing some sort of "mask" to wear? Is it hypocrisy to wear a mask to obscure the facts about the "real me"?

EIGHT

LOVE'S FIRST INSTINCT

Love must be active, or it is meaningless. Throughout this study we have defined love in terms of what it does. Since actions repeated over and over become habitual, we might wonder if love can become a habit. And the answer is, "Yes!" Love can become so habitual in our lives that we do the "loving thing" almost instinctively.

BELIEVING IN PEOPLE

William Barclay was aware of that possibility when he translated 1 Corinthians 13. He renders verse seven this way: "Love's first instinct is to believe in people." Put simply, that means my initial response to a person is to expect the best of that individual. True, some people may later prove themselves undeserving of trust. But I do not let my disappointment with a few make me unduly suspicious of all others.

One of the great tragedies of our day is the low expectation we have of our fellow man. Few people expect businessmen to be honest or political leaders to be above corruption. We even doubt the basic goodness of our neighbors.

We should not be surprised, then, by the ongoing saga of crime and corruption. People have a way of becoming what we expect of them. A child who is expected to fail generally lives up to everyone's expectations. By the same token, a child who is expected to succeed commonly does so. This principle seems valid throughout human society. And *because we as a culture have expected so little of man, he has turned out to be "little" indeed.*

SIGNS OF THE TIMES

Not only do we have a low expectation of others, we seem to enjoy learning that our suspicions about people have been confirmed. One sign of the times is the proliferation of "scandal sheets," those sensationalistic tabloids and periodicals that line magazine racks everywhere. They are prominently displayed at the checkout counters of grocery and department stores, their headlines shouting about the private lives and purported misdeeds of well-known entertainment and political figures. And despite the sordid record such publications have for presenting the facts fairly — or even truthfully — their readership numbers in the millions.

These newspapers and magazines rarely obscure the fact that they are gossip put into print. In fact, there seems to be a growing trend for the word "gossip" to shed its unpleasant overtones. Today a journalist can be proud of the title "Washington gossip columnist." But this attempt to give gossip respectability must never cloud over the danger and the damnability of the practice. Gossip is a serious sin, serious because it chokes back love's first instinct, that of believing in people.

SATAN'S WEAPON

Although gossip (and the attendant failure to believe in people) is a universal illness, let us use the limited space here to note how this illness threatens the kingdom of God. In the church gossip is especially deadly. By sowing distrust and suspicion, it can paralyze the Lord's army. If there

> Because we as a culture have expected so little of man, he has turned out to be "little" indeed.

46

was ever a place where people need to believe in one another, it is in the church. Satan faces no greater foe in the world today than a united church. If he has any intelligence whatsoever, he will throw everything he can at the church. He will do his utmost to plant discord in the fellowship and to discredit spiritual leaders.

> We should never forget that Satan would rather spread his venom among God's people than anywhere else on earth.

Realizing that, we should be all the more eager to exercise love's basic instinct by believing in people. *We should never forget that Satan would rather spread his venom among God's people than anywhere else on earth.* When we hear a "bad report" about a brother in Christ or a sister congregation of the faith, we should immediately suspect that the father of lies is hawking his slander once more.

INNOCENT UNTIL PROVEN GUILTY

Perhaps that is why Paul encouraged Timothy to receive a charge against an elder only when two or three witnesses were available (1 Timothy 5:19). What a good practice for any of us to follow, no matter what Christian is under accusation. In the church, of all places, we must go beyond mere lip service to the principle of considering men innocent until proven guilty. And even when they are proven guilty, we should still continue to believe in them.

That means we have no right to repeat a detracting story about a brother or sister in the Lord, EVEN IF THE STORY IS TRUE. A child of God has stumbled. Should we make it harder for that person by broadcasting the mistake? Is that what we call love? Satan has already scored one point. Shall we help him score another by repeating a story that maligns a fellow Christian? And what of people outside the church? How will their hearing of the incident affect their estimation of Christianity?

If we believe in our brothers and sisters in Christ (and love demands that of us), we have every hope that they will profit from their mistakes and grow spiritually. Refusing to repeat "what we know about them" is one means of producing a favorable climate for that growth. We should also support them with prayers, prayers worded to reflect our confidence in them, not our disappointment. And then we will go a step further by seeking constructive ways to personally aid their spiritual growth.

MATTERS OF OPINION

Thus far, however, our discussion has centered on how love responds to a brother or sister accused of violating explicit commands of God. Yet most problems between brethren do not occur in that realm. The majority of our problems occur in those areas where there is no clear-cut line between what is right and what is wrong. Moral controversies often force the consideration of issues for which there is no clear "thus saith the Lord." For example, we might think of the endless (and often fruitless) debates that have surrounded the question of when and where a Christian can take another's life. Or the related matter of whether a Christian can enter combat. On these, as with thousands of other issues in the life of the church, individual viewpoints will inevitably differ.

How should I react to brothers and sisters who disagree with me on such issues? Have I bought the devil's lie that people who cannot see Scripture the way I do must be my spiritual inferior? How often I am tempted to say, "If he really respected the authority of God's Word, he would understand this exactly the way I do." But statements like that reflect a deep, underlying egotism and self-righteousness. And I can hardly be unconcerned about such attitudes on my part, for the sins associated with self-righteousness are among the most damnable of all.

We must steadily resist Satan's efforts to make me question the spirituality of anyone who reaches conclusions that differ from my own.

48

RESPECTING ONE ANOTHER'S SPIRITUALITY

We must recognize the right of fellow Christians and sister congregations to differ with us on many aspects of Christian living and leadership. Here especially the instinct of believing in people must come to the fore. *We must steadily resist Satan's efforts at this point. He will do his best to make me question the spirituality of anyone who reaches conclusions that differ from my own,* particularly in religious and ethical matters. I must resist the temptation to be suspicious, opting instead to love my fellow Christian and to demonstrate that love by believing in him or her.

Love obligates me to expect the best of those in the family of God, to view them as honest, spiritually-minded disciples who are trying just as hard as I am to do what the Lord expects. Such instinctive belief in others will do more to maintain a strong, harmonious fellowship than almost anything else I can do.

REFLECTING ON LESSON EIGHT

1. Why do you think people are so eager to learn something scandalous about someone else? What motivates such curiosity?

2. Give some examples from day-to-day life that show that we basically do not "believe in people."

3. Is gossip necessarily untrue? Are we justified in repeating a story just because we know it to be true? What guidelines should govern our willingness to repeat a report?

4. Consider two people who are both solid Bible students and respect God's authority. What factors might cause them to draw differing conclusions about the appropriateness of a certain practice? What could cause them to hold different opinions?

5. Give some examples of how Satan can use scandal (whether factual or supposed) to paralyze a church.

6. What Biblical passages can you cite which suggest that our basic responsibility is to build up one another whenever possible?

7. What is the relationship between "believing in people" and patience? Can you cite biblical examples of how someone's patience led to winning over a person?

8. 1 Corinthians 13:7 suggests that love basically thinks of people as good. Do you necessarily agree with that? Are people basically good? Where possible, use biblical references to support your answer.

NINE

LOVE NEVER GIVES UP

One earmark of love is its steadfastness. In chapter three we learned how love is built on a foundation of hope and love. So long as faith perseveres, "love can stand any kind of treatment . . . . Love never regards anything as hopeless; nothing can happen that can break love's spirit" (1 Corinthians 13:7, Barclay's translation).

ULTIMATE WELL-BEING

Worded simply, love never gives up. It so earnestly desires the well-being of the one loved that it strives tirelessly for the best interest of the one it loves. It never quits hoping that things will turn out well for that person. This does not mean that love naively expects every event in the loved one's life to be pleasant. Love fully recognizes that tragedy, misfortune, and pain are inescapable elements of the human condition. But it also recognizes that the present condition of man is a temporary one, that he is intended for a destiny that transcends suffering and death. Thus, love does not let its attention become fixed on temporary things, whether those things be pleasant or unpleasant. Instead, love's primary interest is the *ultimate* and *eternal* well-being of the loved one.

51

REJECTED LOVE

Pursuit of another's well-being may turn out to be a thankless task. Love realizes that. It is prepared to endure all things, even rejection by the one loved. *Mature loves does not demand "repayment in kind." That is, it does not love so that it can be loved in return.*

No mother in her right mind abandons her infant child because the child shows no evidence of returning the mother's love. Through dirty diapers, sleepless nights, and endless bottle washings the mother continues to love. For weeks after its birth the child will show only rudimentary responses, none of which could be genuinely called "acts of love." But the mother's love remains constant, not caring whether love is returned or not.

So it is with friends. What kind of friendship would say, "I will continue to be your friend only so long as you treat me properly"? Such a statement indicates immature love, a self-serving love, not a love that seeks the well-being of the other. How easy it would have been for Jesus, on the night when Peter denied Him, to have said, "When Peter changes and begins to act like a friend, then I will be ready to love him again." But instead of that typically human response, Jesus saw to it that His own love continued steadfast, even when Peter's love failed. The perseverance of Jesus' love, even in the face of disappointment, must have been a key to Peter's eventual reclamation.

LOOKING BEYOND THE PRESENT

Jesus' love, then, is the love that does not give up. The power of its steadfastness is its ability to look beyond the present moment, even if the present moment represents denial and betrayal by a friend. Looking beyond the moment, such love searches for the *ultimate* well-being of the one loved; then, having fixed its gaze on those ultimate interests, love is prepared to endure all things.

> **Mature loves does not demand "repayment in kind." That is, it does not love so that it can be loved in return.**

Nor does love *resent* being called on to forbear with a friend, even a faithless one. *Love that resents is not genuine love. Resentment indicates that love is still seeking its own interests.* It still wants to focus on itself and its own rights. It wants to keep track of the "impositions" that have been placed on it by friendship. But it is impossible to impose on mature love, for it willingly surrenders its privileges in order to bear with the one loved. Thus, William Barclay translated 1 Corinthians 13:5 as, "Love never does the graceless thing; never insists on its rights."

INVESTMENTS, NOT SACRIFICE

There is a second sense, therefore, in which "love never gives up." Since love does not keep track of impositions, it never concerns itself with "what I have given up for the beloved." Love that maintains an inventory of what it has had to "give up" is hardly worthy of the name love. Mature love sees its patience, its prayers, and its pain not so much as sacrifice as an investment. Because love "hopes all things," it has every expectation that its investment will return great dividends. Thus, love never views itself as giving *up* anything. It only looks at itself as giving *to* the enterprise of loving, an enterprise that will return great dividends.

THE PITFALL

But there is a danger here. Love cannot afford to let itself focus on the return it will eventually collect. Once love does that, it reverts back to an immature form of love. It becomes self-serving again, a love still I-centered and not genuinely you-centered. What an irony!! The secret of love's endurance is its ability to see beyond the moment to the ultimate outcome; yet, if love begins looking for its own interests in that ultimate outcome, it ceases to be love! When love looks at the final outcome of the loving enterprise, it sees not so much what it will itself receive, but what the loved one will acquire. And having dedicated itself to the ultimate well-being of the beloved, love pledges itself never to give up until that end is at hand.

REFLECTING ON LESSON NINE

1. What is meant by the term "self-seeking love"?

2. Explain this statement: "At no moment is it more important for love to persevere than at the moment love is rejected."

3. Give examples of how God's love has persevered, even when His love was rejected. Include some instances when His forbearance eventually bore fruit.

4. Can you cite at least two biblical examples of a love that never gave up?

5. How can a person overcome his resentment of what he has to "give up" for a friend? Give practical suggestions.

6. Can I really determine what I need to do right now to further the "ultimate and eternal well-being" of a neighbor? Or do I just "wing it" and hope things work out well in the long run? Are there ever moments when it is appropriate to promote the short-term well-being of another, even though we may believe that such action does not serve the needs of his long-term well-being?

10
T E N

LOVE FULFILLS THE LAW

In today's religious market it is not uncommon for someone to merchandise the idea that grace and law are opposed to one another. Romans and Galatians are favorite "proving grounds" for this theory. But Romans and Galatians do not address themselves to the relationship between law and grace per se. Instead, these books concern themselves with the difference between salvation by faith and salvation by works. They draw the contrast between a person who is seeking salvation by faith in God's grace and the person who is seeking to be saved merely by doing the works of God's law. While it is true that *salvation* by works is opposed to *salvation* by grace, it does not necessarily follow that law and grace are *themselves* opposed to one another.

GRACE AND LAW

Everyone agrees, for instance, that preaching the gospel means declaring "the grace of God has appeared, bringing salvation to all men" (Titus 2:11). But some want us to stop there, preaching only salvation through grace. To these people it is a corruption of the gospel to preach that grace obligates us to keep certain spiritual and moral laws. Yet Paul himself said,

We know that the Law is good, if one uses it lawfully, realizing the fact that law is not made for a righteous man, but for those who are lawless and rebellious, for the ungodly and sinners, for the unholy and profane, for those who kill fathers or mothers, for murderers and immoral men and homosexuals and kidnappers and liars and perjurers, and whatever else is contrary to sound teaching *according to the glorious gospel of the blessed God* (1 Timothy 1:8-11, emphasis added).

So preaching the gospel *does* include the proclamation of certain divine laws that are to be respected and obeyed.

LAW'S LIMITATION

Law, however, has one great limitation. If it is to be easily learned, the body of law must be concise. But if it is concise, it cannot be extensive enough to include specific guidelines for every situation. There will always come times when those who are under the law will have to interpret the law for themselves. This is especially the case when they find themselves in a situation where they cannot keep one law without violating another.

Such was the dilemma of the Hebrew midwives in Exodus 1, women who were forced either to lie or to be accessories to murder (Exodus 1:15-21). Rahab the harlot, 120 years later, found herself in the same predicament (Joshua 2:1-7). At such a moment of crisis, how do I know which commandment to keep and which to set aside?

THE PURPOSE OF THE LAW

Paul gives the answer in that now famous dictum, "Love fulfills the law" (See Romans 13:8-10). We might elaborate on this statement with the addition of one clarifying word: *"Love fulfills the* intent *of the law."* God's law, as Paul told Timothy, is not evil, but good. To the Romans, Paul also described the law as "holy and righteous and good" (Romans 7:12). *God ordained His laws not to diminish human well-being, but to promote it.* Our primary concern, therefore,

Love fulfills the *intent* of the law.

56

should not be the letter of the law, but the intent of the law. And if keeping the *letter* of the law would go against human well-being in a particular circumstance, we would violate the *intent* of the law by keeping the letter.

God ordained His laws not to diminish human well-being, but to promote it.

MAN FOR THE SABBATH

That is what Jesus meant when He said, "Man was not made for the Sabbath, but the Sabbath for man" (Mark 2:22, author's paraphrase). Throughout His ministry Jesus was accused of being disrespectful of God's law concerning the Sabbath. The specific charge laid against him was healing on the Sabbath. But His defense was always the same: if keeping the letter of the law meant leaving a fellow human to suffer, the letter of the law must be set aside in favor of the *purpose* of the law.

Jesus pursued this same line of reasoning when His disciples were accused of gathering grain on the Sabbath. He reminded his accusers that David and his troops had justifiably eaten the shewbread, a deed clearly unacceptable under Mosaic law. But the hunger of David's men — as well as the hunger of Jesus' disciples — demanded that the letter of the law be suspended so that the well-being of man might be pursued (Matthew 12:1-14; 1 Samuel 21:1-6).

WHAT DOES LOVE DEMAND?

These stories illustrate boldly the principle that Paul enunciated: love fulfills the meaning of the law. Whenever I find myself in a circumstance where God's moral and spiritual laws have not given me explicit guidelines, I must somehow interpret the meaning of the law for such a circumstance. The way I go about determining that meaning is by asking the question, "What does love demand in this instance?" Since love is an "active and genuine concern for the well-being of the loved one," *the pursuit of love's interests will never be opposed to the intentions of divine law.*

Paul put it this way:

Owe nothing to anyone except to love one another; for he who loves his neighbor has fulfilled the law. For this, 'YOU SHALL NOT COMMIT ADULTERY, YOU SHALL NOT STEAL, YOU SHALL NOT COVET,' and if there is any other commandment, it is summed up in this saying, 'YOU SHALL LOVE YOUR NEIGHBOR AS YOURSELF.' Love does no wrong to a neighbor; love therefore is the fulfillment of the law (Romans 13:8-10).

A CONTRAST WITH SITUATION ETHICS

This position is not situation ethics, however. Those who advocate situation ethics have properly noted the biblical principle that there are times when the letter of the law must be set aside in the interest of humanitarianism. Like most false teachers, however, they have taken a valid biblical viewpoint to an unholy extreme.

Classical situation ethics says that I have a right to set aside God's law anytime I would not hurt anyone by doing so. The biblical viewpoint is much more restrained. It says that I have the right to set aside God's law *ONLY* if demanding the letter of the law would work against the principles of love. Put more simply, situation ethics says that I do not have to *keep* the law unless I would bring manifest harm to someone by *breaking* it. Christian ethics says I cannot *break* the law unless I would bring manifest harm to someone by *holding to its letter*.

The pursuit of love's interests will never be opposed to the intentions of divine law.

REFLECTING ON LESSON TEN

1. Explain what is meant by the statement, "The law is good and holy." How does law aid mankind's well-being?

2. Elaborate on the significance of Jesus' statement, "The Sabbath was made for man, not man for the Sabbath."

3. Explain how the law is summed up in the command, "You shall love your neighbor as yourself."

4. Do you think the Egyptian midwives followed the right course in Exodus 1? How can you explain the statement that "God blessed the midwives" when they had so blatantly misrepresented the truth (Exodus 1:20)?

5. Why is love interested in the spirit of the law and not the letter?

6. An early Christian writer said, "Love God and do as you please." His point was that when we truly love God, what will please us is doing His will. Do you agree?

7. Describe some circumstances in which a Christian may have to determine whether the literal keeping of God's law would work against the spirit of God's law.

ELEVEN

FAITH WORKING THROUGH LOVE

People who love are fearless! That does not mean they are never frightened. To the contrary, fear may often seize them. But unlike those who are paralyzed by fear, loving people are able to push their fears aside and act decisively. As the apostle John said, "Perfect love casts out fear" (1 John 4:18). Moreover, the Christian, through his faith, escapes many of the fears that plague others. The love of God has delivered them from the fear of death, for "there is therefore now no condemnation for those who are in Christ Jesus" (Romans 8:1). In addition, their love of their fellow man has delivered them from the fear of God's judgment, for "he who loves his neighbor has fulfilled the law" (Romans 13:8).

UNSHRINKING FAITH

This "perfect love" which casts out fear is the end product of faith. We have seen in chapter three that the hope produced by faith yields patience, graciousness, contentment — in short, all the qualities of love. It is no surprise, therefore, that not only love, but faith, too, is pictured as overcoming fear. John said, "This is the victory that has overcome the world, — our faith" (1 John 5:4). And the Hebrew writer, warning against shrinking back in fear, added, "We are not of those who shrink back and are lost; we have the faith to make life our own" (Hebrews 10:37-39, NEB). The person who "shrinks back," then, is not yet "living by faith."

FRUITS OF FEAR

No great perception is required to see what a vast gulf separates a life of fear from a life of love. Look at the qualities that characterize fear: nervousness, anxiety, uncertainty, worry, hesitation, doubt, even panic. Recall the man in chapter one who, standing outside his neighbor's burning house, learned that a small child was still inside. At that moment fear of the flames told him to hesitate. Uncertain whether he could make it into the house and out again safely, unable to know if his efforts would be of any avail, he might well have been convinced to stand and watch hopelessly. And that's the key word — *hopelessly*!!

Fearful people are hopeless people. Even though they *speak* of hoping for the best, their hopes are not grounded in confidence and assurance. Nowhere is there a clearer contrast between lives of fear and lives of love than in the abject hopelessness of the former and the unshakable hope of the latter.

Because of this difference between fearful men and loving men, the story in chapter one did not end with the neighbor standing outside the burning home, watching while a child perished. Not at all! His "perfect love cast out fear," and with determination he dashed into the flames! Because of his love he did not "shrink back."

IMITATION CHRISTIANITY

Fearlessness and love, therefore, go hand in hand. Their presence produces fruit that distinguishes the Christian from the non-Christian. For that reason, James wrote that "faith, if it has no works, is dead, being by itself" (James 2:17). *If faith is complete, it yields a quality of fearlessness and love that cannot be missed* when people observe our conduct. This is not to say there are no cheap imitations of Christianity floating around. Quite the contrary, there *are* those who, for whatever reasons, try to duplicate in their lives all the "works" of Christianity. They may even keep up the masquerade for prolonged periods. But if we watch them closely enough and long enough, their real colors eventually show through. In time their deep-seated fearfulness and hopelessness will let itself be known.

That is why Paul, in both Romans and Galatians, insists that we put our efforts into duplicating the faith, not the works, of righteousness. When our faith is what it should be, we will not have to worry about our works. *When our hearts are fearless and loving, the proper works — what Paul calls the fruit of the Spirit — will flow naturally and fully from our lives.* This is because our hearts control our bodies, and not vice versa. My body may go through the "motions" of Christianity for years, even decades, but those motions will not make wholesale change in my heart. On the other hand, the very moment my heart begins to be influenced by the gospel, an immediate and observable change reflects itself in my behavior.

CHANGE THE INNER MAN

The Russian actor Stanislovsky, the father of method acting, recognized this principle. He taught his students that the key to effective acting lay in duplicating the feelings and state of mind of the person portrayed. If you are going to portray a bum, he would say, go live with the bums long enough you learn what it feels like to be a bum. Then, when you step onto stage, recreate that feeling in your heart and the rest will take care of itself. Your stance, your gestures, even your facial muscles will be transformed into the posture and appearance of a bum.

Amateur actors are so preoccupied with the way they are moving their hands, the way they have positioned their feet, the way they are speaking

> When our hearts are fearless and loving, the fruit of the Spirit will flow naturally and fully from our lives.

their lines — so preoccupied, that is, with the *externals* of their performance — that they never recreate the inner feelings that are part of genuine portrayals. Even so, *"amateur Christians" allow themselves to become so absorbed with the externals, the "works" of Christianity, that they fail to engraft the love of God into their hearts.* Thus, Paul warns such amateurs about the worthlessness of such externals. What avails itself in Christianity, he said, is faith that works through love (Galatians 5:6).

"Amateur Christians" allow themselves to become so absorbed with the externals that they fail to engraft the love of God into their hearts.

SERVING FEARLESSLY

To put this another way, the quality of our work for the Lord is a product of the quality of our love. Until our love perfects itself to the casting out of fear, our work will be little more than an "on today, off tomorrow" series of hesitations. Love's power to cast out fear yields the unshakable hope that faith brings in its train. When I am *really convinced* of the Christian hope, when I am *really convinced* that God's promises are true, I will not shrink back, no matter the duty that love demands.

Whatever the task, I will act fearlessly! As a young man once said to me, "If I know I am living for eternity, I can face *anything* the world throws at me for 80 years."

REFLECTING ON LESSON ELEVEN

1. What characteristics distinguish the person of fear from the person of faith?

2. How does "perfect love cast out fear"?

3. If we are not saved by works, why are Christian works so important?

4. Why does God say in Hebrews 10:38 that He has no pleasure in the person who "shrinks back"?

5. Can "perfect love" help a person overcome shyness? Is it possible to have "perfect love" and lack self-confidence?

6. It has been suggested that human beings have six basic fears. Which of the following do you think is the greatest fear? Which the least? How does "perfect love" help us overcome each of these specific fears?
   a. fear of poverty
   b. fear of criticism
   c. fear of ill health
   d. fear of losing someone dear
   e. fear of old age
   f. fear of death

12
T W E L V E

LOVE COVERS A MULTITUDE OF SINS

Love is powerful! Yet her power is quiet and unpretentious, like that of a small stream rippling gently over granite boulders. To the observer the water seems without strength, being endlessly diverted by the obstinance of the stone. But over the years an amazing thing happens. The rocks that once stood so defiantly are now gone! And the stream that once brushed tenderly along the face of the earth has now eroded a deep canyon into the bedrock.

Love's tender affection likewise brushes against the boulders of bigotry and bitterness in the world, seeming never to make an impression. Yet, eventually love's perseverance proves decisive. Love thus goes about her work confidently, quietly, patiently. Once she loses her composed and confident patience, she is doomed to failure. But if she refuses to set limitations on her willingness to forgive, if she pledges herself to an endless show of mercy, no force on earth can resist her forever.

SEVENTY TIMES SEVEN

That was the point Jesus was making to his disciples when they asked how many times they should forgive a man. Was seven times enough? No, Jesus answered. They should forgive seventy times seven (Matthew 18:21-22). He did not mean that forgiveness can stop after the 490th sin. Instead He was using a figure of speech to show that *love can cover a multitude of sins, for love never quits wanting to forgive.* That is the secret of its power.

WEARING LOVE OUT

The Danish philosopher Søren Kierkegaard once depicted this power of love in almost poetic language. Whenever sin maliciously slandered love, he wrote, love returned a kindness. Whenever sin enviously hated love, love pronounced a blessing. Whenever sin demanded love's coat, love freely pitched in a shirt as well. Sin finally decided, therefore, that the only way to rid itself of love was to sin against it enough times to wear love out. So sin intentionally did everything possible to cause love to fail. But, said Kierkegaard, sin sooner became tired of needing forgiveness than love did of forgiving.

Such is the love that covers a multitude of sins: a love which, while carefully avoiding the snares of sin, will itself remain eager to forgive long after sin has wearied of needing forgiveness. Could that have been part of what Jesus had in mind when He encouraged His disciples to be "wise as serpents and as harmless as doves" (Matthew 10:16, KJV)?

THE COAT OF CORRUPTION

The quiet confidence that empowers love is anchored in her instinctive belief in people. As we discussed in chapter eight, love expects the best of others. Knowing that the human race began in the image of God, love believes mankind capable of godliness. The obvious and blatant sinfulness of men and women is not their original nature. It is their corrupted nature. And love knows that if she can wear away that coating of corruption, the nobility of the original creation will come shining

> Love can cover a multitude of sins, for love never quits wanting to forgive.

through. That realization is the heart of her patience and the core of her mercy.

In her effort to strip men of their sinful habits, love could be tempted to use a sledgehammer approach. But that would run the risk of shattering the beauty underneath. When an archaeologist sets about unearthing a valuable artifact, he does not employ an air hammer. His tools are small, soft brushes and fine needles with which to remove the encrusted earth. His work is painstaking and slow. But the beauty that fills museums around the world attests to the value of his patience.

> Amateurish and immature love wants to work only with blemish-free stones, unable to see why a man like Jesus would waste His time on publicans and sinners.

THE BEAUTY BELOW

That is why Paul began his description of love by saying, "Love is patient with people; love is kind." Our patience and kindness come from our ability to see beyond the ugliness in a person's life to the beauty underneath. Michelangelo once found a piece of discarded marble, rejected by fellow sculptors because of a jagged crack in the stone. Taking the marble, he skillfully carved around the crack and fashioned his renowned statue of David. What lesser men had seen as only a worthless piece of stone became in the hands of a more perceptive artist an immortal masterwork.

Amateurish and immature love wants to work only with blemish-free stones, unable to see why a man like Jesus would waste His time on publicans and sinners. But Jesus, being the master craftsman, did not allow His attention to be distracted by the superficial ugliness of people. Instead, he perceived the underlying beauty of their image. He came to save sinners, and the only way to do so was to love them — love them despite their chronic sinfulness and their spiritual ugliness.

REFLECTING ON LESSON TWELVE

1. What was the significance of Jesus using seventy times seven to indicate how often we should forgive?

2. What are the sources of love's quiet confidence?

3. Why is it important for love to be gentle with people?

4. Who are the most difficult people for you to love?

5. Give examples from Jesus' ministry when He saw beneath the surface of someone's life and envisioned the beautiful inner potential of that individual.

6. Does the statement "love covers a multitude of sins" ever mean "my love negates the guilt of my personal sins?" If not, why not?

7. What are the most important qualities for love to manifest if it is going to wear down sin?

13

THIRTEEN

LOVE MAKES NO DISTINCTIONS

The early church was a hodgepodge of people from all over the Mediterranean world. Roman centurions, Greek slaves, and converted Jewish rabbis rubbed shoulders with one another at Christian services. Only a loving fellowship had room in it for people of such diverse viewpoints and backgrounds. It was important, therefore, that early Christians learn to avoid making distinctions among believers. James warned them about giving prominent seats to wealthy men, while relegating poor men to the status of footstools (James 2:1-4). Paul had to confront Peter before the entire congregation because of Peter's blatant racism (Galatians 2:11-14). Even the first appointment of deacons was prompted by inequities in a benevolence program that had become class conscious (Acts 6:1-6).

CHRISTIANITY AND SOCIALISM

The apostolic leaders constantly struggled against any sign of preferential treatment based on racial, social, political, economic, or sexual differences. The church did not try to *destroy* those distinctions. It merely *ignored* them. That is the basic difference between the "equality" of ancient Christianity and the "equality" of many modern socialist movements. Both stress the equal and inalienable rights of the individual. But contemporary efforts often try to attain equality by obliterating as many differences as possible. These movements make a concerted effort to bring everyone to the same level, particularly the same economic level. Even sexual distinctions face a serious challenge today. It has been observed, for instance, that some women's rights campaigns are not seeking *equality* with men. They are often seeking *sameness* with men.

LIKENESS, NOT EQUALITY

Perhaps we should more accurately refer to these modern-day movements as efforts to create "likeness" rather than "equality." This likeness is achieved by pulling the poverty-stricken up and pulling the patrician down. A desirable "average" is found, and everyone is forced to conform to that norm.

Christianity, on the other hand, sets its "norm," not at some intermediate level between the height of affluence and the depths of poverty, but at a level higher than the richest of kings. Whether we are princes or paupers, God's standard for us is more lofty than any man has ever achieved: "Therefore you are to be perfect, as your heavenly Father is perfect" (Matthew 5:48). Christianity is not concerned with eliminating distinctions among people. It accepts those distinctions, but then calls on us to rise above our distinctions. *Because "all have sinned and fall short of the glory of God" (Romans 3:23), all men are equals.*

Focusing on that equality, Christian love leaves no room for the rich to be arrogant or the poor to be envious. We are all sinners. Why should I be proud? Because I am a sinner? Ultimately and eternally we are all the same. Some will be saved and others will be lost; but other than that, the only distinctions among human beings are temporal, temporary. Therefore, since love is eternal, it should be practiced without distinctions, for there are no *eternal* distinctions.

Because all have sinned and fall short of the glory of God, all men are equals.

70

"DISTINCTIONLESS" LOVE

We might look to God as an example of this "distinctionless" love. God has never taken sides in any class struggle. Because He created us as individually independent beings, He recognizes that there will always be differences and distinctions among us. God accepts people as they are, ignoring the class a person happens to be in. Greeks and gangsters, bankers and blasphemers, princes and prostitutes are all accepted on the same basis. God never required a slave to gain his freedom before becoming a Christian. And He never required a king to relinquish His throne before receiving grace. Instead, He treated them both as sinners and equals, reconciling both according to the same plan of salvation.

The Bible never attacks a person just because he is rich, no more than it praises someone because he happens to be poor.

THE BIBLE AND THE RICH MAN

God's refusal to take sides in class struggles may not be immediately obvious. That is because the Bible speaks so sympathetically of the poor and so scathingly of the rich. When asked what the Bible teaches about rich men, most people will immediately respond that "it is harder for a rich man to go to heaven than for a camel to go through the eye of a needle" (Matthew 19:24, author's paraphrase). We overlook the fact that Abraham, the father of the faithful, was so wealthy and preeminent that he was frequently the guest of pharaohs and kings. Job, the epitome of godly patience, was a man of incalculable wealth. And David, a builder of empires and a resplendent capital, was a man after God's own heart.

The Bible never attacks a person just because he is rich, no more than it praises someone because he happens to be poor. It does speak out against riches improperly acquired. And it speaks with equal fury against the man with "this world's goods" who refuses to meet his neighbor's needs. But it looks not so much at a person's bank account as at his heart, not so much

71

at his accumulations as his generosity. A man with immense wealth may give it all away to feed the poor. Yet, if he does so without love, it profits him nothing (1 Corinthians 13:3). Thus, the only thing that "makes a difference" is the heart of a person.

LOVE DOESN'T MAKE ANY DIFFERENCE

God, through the cross of Jesus, seems to have underscored the "distinctionless" nature of love. As was prophesied, Jesus made His grave with the rich and the poor. Crucified between thieves, He was taken down to be laid in the tomb of an aristocrat. *Thus, He died as He had lived, making no distinctions as to "suitable company."* His love — and hence his death — went out to all people. That does not mean that He was blind to human distinctions. He was *intensely* aware of them. But He left for us the perfect pattern of love, a love that can say, "The differences between people don't make any difference to me. I will love every person, one and all."

Jesus died as He had lived, making no distinctions as to "suitable company."

72

REFLECTING ON LESSON THIRTEEN

1. Show how Jesus, during His ministry, made no distinctions in His love.

2. List the problems that existed in the early church because people tried to set up distinctions within the fellowship.

3. Contrast the "equality" of Christianity with the "equality" of socialism.

4. Give some biblical examples of God's people ignoring distinctions that were commonly honored among men.

5. How do you answer the critic who says that Christianity, by refusing to work toward the eradication of distinctions among classes, is really a non-humanitarian religion?

6. Is God's standard realistic when He says, "You be perfect as I am perfect"?

7. If God does not respect persons, why does He allow some to become wealthy and others to remain poor within the same church?